Killer Ants

Written by Anna Porter

Illustrated by Alex Stitt

Flying Start
to Literacy®

T0363499

CONTENTS

Chapter 1
What's happening in the jungle?   4

Chapter 2
Where is my baby?   12

Chapter 3
Where is my mother?   16

Chapter 4
Save me!   20

CHAPTER 1
What's happening in the jungle?

There was panic in the jungle. The animals were running and crying out in fear.

The snakes and monkeys raced quickly through the treetops.

The gorillas leaped over the grass.

The elephants charged across the jungle floor, crashing through trees and breaking branches.

The animals were running to the
river because they had heard a
terrifying noise. It was the noise
of an army of ants. Hundreds of
ants, thousands of ants, millions
and millions of ants.

CRICK!

The driver ants were marching
through the jungle, looking for food
and a place to build a new nest.

In the river the animals would be
safe from the ants because the ants
could not swim.

A huge army of ants, 25 metres wide and five metres deep, was marching through the jungle. The ants were destroying all before them.

Ants with sharp, biting jaws.
Ants that were ready to eat
any animal foolish enough to cross
their path. Ants that could strip
small animals to their bones
in minutes.

People fled too. They picked up
their children and ran.

Jungle workers grabbed their tools
and ran out of the jungle, away
from the army of driver ants.

CHAPTER 2
Where is my baby?

As the animals fled the jungle,
one animal started to run the
wrong way.

The mother gorilla had lost her baby.
She ran back into the jungle, past
the old fallen tree
and up the hill.

She ran towards the marching
ants, towards the hundreds
and thousands and millions
of biting jaws.

As the mother gorilla ran she called
and screeched. She had to find
her baby before the ants got to him.

Then she saw him. At the top of
the hill, the young gorilla was
playing, right in the path of the
driver ants.

The young gorilla didn't know about driver ants. He heard the sound made by the millions of ants marching through the jungle, but he did not know what it was.

The ants marched closer and closer and closer.

CRICK?
CRICK?

CHAPTER 3
Where is my mother?

Then the young gorilla heard his mother calling to him. He looked around, but he couldn't see her anywhere.

But he saw the ants – hundreds of ants, thousands of ants, millions and millions of ants, marching towards him.

Suddenly he was afraid.   He turned to run – but which way should he go?

The baby gorilla was terrified.
He did not know what to do or
where to go.

He fell on the ground, put his
head under his arm and started
to cry. He wanted his mother.

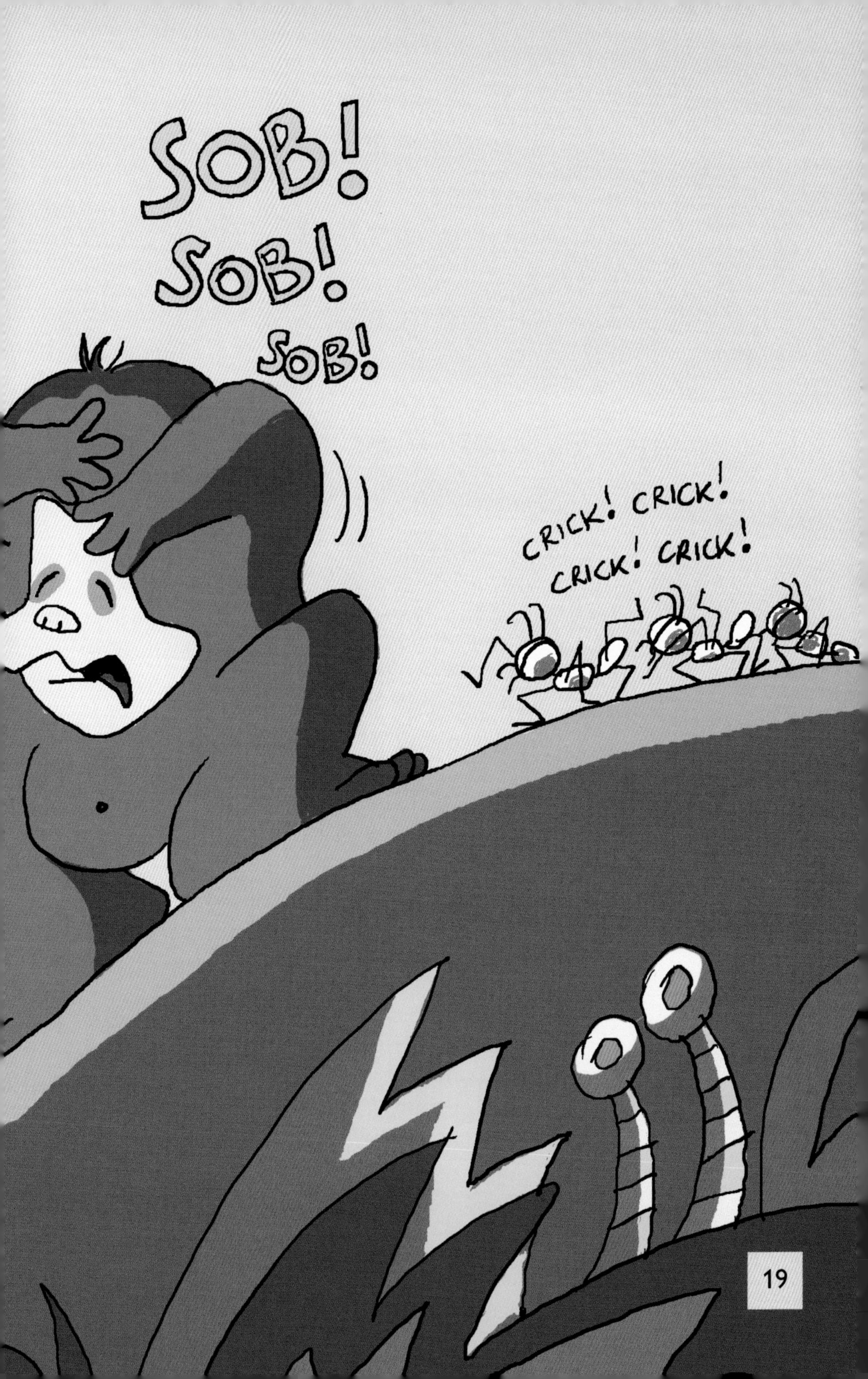
SOB!
SOB!
SOB!
CRICK! CRICK!
CRICK! CRICK!

CHAPTER 4
Save me!

At that moment his mother was
there beside him. She scooped
him up and put him on her back.

And then she ran back through the jungle. She ran away from the ants, away from the millions of biting jaws and marching feet.

The mother gorilla ran down the hill but the ants kept marching – hundreds of ants, thousands of ants, millions and millions of ants.

She ran past the old fallen tree,
but the ants kept marching.

Then the mother gorilla saw
the river.

CRICK! CRICK! CRICK! CRICK!

CRICK! CRICK! CRICK!

CRICK!

RICK!

CRICK! CRICK!
CRICK!

The mother gorilla plunged into
the river with her baby.

They were safe in the river,
where the ants could not go.